Take a Look!
Modern Media Literacy

Identifying the Source

I0886428

Julie Knutson

Cherry Lake Press

Published in the United States of America by Cherry Lake Publishing Group
Ann Arbor, Michigan
www.cherrylakepublishing.com

Reading Adviser: Beth Walker Gambro, MS, Ed., Reading Consultant, Yorkville, IL
Content Adviser: Kristin Fontichiaro, Clinical Professor, University of Michigan School of Information

Photo Credits: © Andrii Iemelianenko/Shutterstock, cover, title page; © BCTumSS/Shutterstock, 5; © Mergeldea/Shutterstock, 6; © DC Studio/Shutterstock, 7; © Jacob Lund/Shutterstock, 8; © T. Schneider/Shutterstock, 9; © Ascannio/Shutterstock, 10; © Hananeko_Studio/Shutterstock, 11; © SpeedKingz/Shutterstock, 12; © Louiza Houache/Shutterstock, 13; 15; 17; © mimagephotography/Shutterstock, 18; © Kafka Ibram/Shutterstock, 19; © The KonG/Shutterstock, 20; © EF Stock/Shuterstock, 21; © mimagephotography/Shutterstock, 22; © Poetra.RH/Shutterstock, 23; © Stivog/Shutterstock, 25; © Pixel-Shot/Shutterstock, 26; © pics five/Shutterstock, 27; © Prostock-studio/Shutterstock, 28; © Wayhome Studio/Shutterstock, 30; © pics five/Shutterstock, 31

Copyright © 2025 by Cherry Lake Publishing Group

All rights reserved. No part of this book may be reproduced or utilized in any form or by any means without written permission from the publisher.

Cherry Lake Press is an imprint of Cherry Lake Publishing Group.

Library of Congress Cataloging-in-Publication Data

Names: Knutson, Julie, author.
Title: Identifying the source / written by Julie Knutson.
Description: Ann Arbor, Michigan : Cherry Lake Publishing, 2025. | Series: Take a look! Modern media literacy | Audience: Grades 4-6 | Summary: "Part of our Take a Look! Modern Media Literacy series, Identifying the Source takes readers through the process of analyzing media in order to tell fact from fiction. Includes explanation of how misinformation, disinformation, biases, and stereotypes play into the credibility of a source. Gives readers the information they need to start practicing looking critically at the media they consume. Series closely aligned with standards from the American Association of School Librarians and the Journalism Education Association. This series gives readers a crash course in basic media literacy skills: understanding audience, perspective, persuasive appeals, author's purpose, tracing sources, and creating media content"—Provided by publisher.
Identifiers: LCCN 2024035930 | ISBN 9781668956311 (hardcover) | ISBN 9781668957165 (paperback) | ISBN 9781668958032 (ebook) | ISBN 9781668958902 (pdf)
Subjects: LCSH: Media literacy—Juvenile literature. | Information resources—Evaluation—Juvenile literature. | Critical thinking—Juvenile literature. | Misinformation—Juvenile literature. | Disinformation—Juvenile literature. | Mass media—Objectivity—Juvenile literature.
Classification: LCC P96.M4 K58 2025 | DDC 302.23—dc23/eng/20240827
LC record available at https://lccn.loc.gov/2024035930

Cherry Lake Press would like to acknowledge the work of the Partnership for 21st Century Learning, a Network of Battelle for Kids. Please visit Battelle for Kids online for more information.

Printed in the United States of America

Note from publisher: Websites change regularly, and their future contents are outside of our control. Supervise children when conducting any recommended online searches for extended learning opportunities.

Julie Knutson (she/her) is an author and educator who lives and works in Philadelphia, PA. She's no stranger to navigating media in our modern world, and she teaches her students to do the same. Whether working with students to craft interview questions or debating designs for a classroom magazine, she also loves guiding middle schoolers through the media-making process.

CONTENTS

CHAPTER 1

Take a Look! The Big Picture

Television. The internet. Radio, social media, magazines, newspapers, blogs. Class discussions and podcasts. Family, friends, and teachers.

The list of ways to learn about our world is *long*. Different forms of **media**—and the people around us—may provide us with information. But how can you tell if the creator, or **source**, of the information is reliable? How can you find trustworthy sources? And how can you trace information back to its source?

Where do kids and teens get their news? The authors of *Breaking the News* surveyed children ages 10 to18. They found that 49 percent of respondents said that social media and the internet kept them up to speed on current events.

Over 240 million people use Twitch every month.

Abby is looking for a new video game. She follows gamers on Twitch. She follows gamers on Instagram. These gamer influencers have thousands of followers. One of the influencers recommends a new game Abby hasn't heard of before. She finds it online and buys it. It turns out not to be a great fit for Abby.

A big part of knowing how to navigate media involves knowing yourself. You get to decide if media is a good fit for you or not—whether it's a game review or the game itself.

Sometimes it's hard to spot ads. But if a video has #ad, #partnership, or #sponsored, it's definitely an ad.

THINK & CURATE

Curate means to carefully select. It's important to know how to curate your sources when you're creating media. It's important that you choose reliable sources. How do you determine whose work you trust? What questions do you ask when looking for good sources?

A few weeks later, she sees a new video from the same gamer. The gamer is recommending another game. Abby reads the text under the video. She sees "#ad" and realizes this is a paid partnership. The gamer gets paid to recommend certain games. Abby finds the original post for the game she bought—it was an ad, too! Abby wonders if she would have made a different decision had she known.

Not long after, one of Abby's friends recommends a game they've been playing. This friend recommends the game because they enjoy it. They thought Abby would like it. There's no other reason. Abby wonders if she should ask her friends first next time!

Abby has learned an important lesson. Different people and media companies have different goals. They may create and change media to support their goals on purpose.

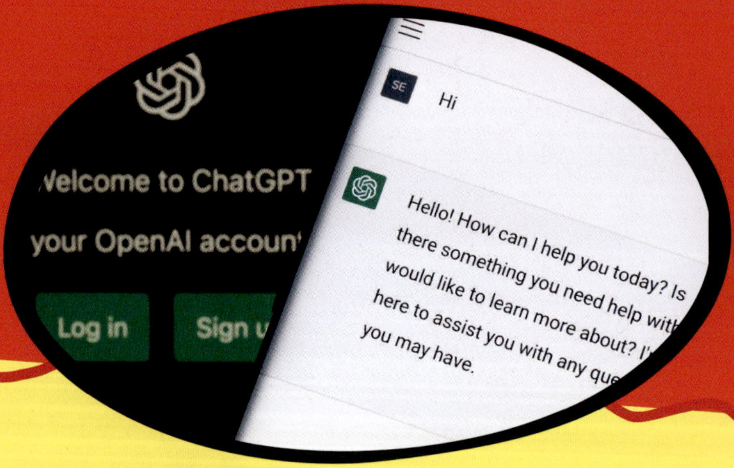

GROW & ENGAGE

Do you think of AI as a source? AI can generate knowledge in different ways, including sounds, pictures, and text. Is there a right way for AI to do this? Is there a wrong way? What concerns do some people have about AI content? How could people use AI content in a responsible way?

Abby chose to ask her friend for a recommendation. Now they get to enjoy media together!

Today, information swirls around us. It can be hard to tell fact from fiction. We can also easily forget that information comes from *people*. Stopping to ask, "Who made this?" "What was their perspective?" and "Why did they create it?" is important. These questions make us conscious that there's a human behind everything we see, hear, and read.

Always double-check any information you get from an AI source. Don't trust it right away!

WHAT'S THE "SOURCE" BEHIND AI?

AI is trained—or programmed—by **engineers**. AI "knows" what it knows because of engineers. They feed it information from vast banks of data. Where does AI get its information? It's often the internet.

This brings us to a problem. Some people post information online that is false.

AI data comes from many sources—so many that they are often untraceable or unreliable. The data that gets gathered may be false information. The programming of the software that takes in and sorts this data was made by people. People have different viewpoints and values. Both the data and the software may have been made by people with strong **biases**. That could spread **stereotypes**.

Behind every machine—just like every piece of media—there's a person. With all things AI-generated, pause. Ask hard questions about what you're seeing or reading—and where it came from.

CHAPTER 2

Break It Down! Smart Source Sleuthing

We know the *why* of source sleuthing. But where do you start? Once you find a source, how do you confirm it's reliable?

Meet Nur. Nur is a curious middle schooler. Right now, he's obsessed with Taylor Swift. He's new to the world of Swifties. He needs to learn more about Swift in order to join fan conversations. He decides to find more information about her online.

He wants to be able to weed out creators he doesn't trust.

Nur is excited to learn more about his favorite pop star. But he needs to find a source he can trust. Otherwise, he'll look bad in front of the other Swifties.

He comes up with the following questions to vet his sources.

- Is this source an expert?
- Where did they get their information?
- Will this source make money from the content? How does the company or person who created this make their money?

Nur chooses to search on Instagram for some more information on Swift. He finds an account called *Page Eight* with a post about her. Under her picture, it says she hinted that she's releasing a new album. Wow! Nur is so excited. He wants to look more closely at the source. He goes through his questions:

- **Is this source an expert?**

  He looks at the top of the page. There is a blue checkmark next to the account name. That means it's verified. A source could be more trustworthy if it's verified. He looks at the bio at the top of the *Page Eight* profile. It says, "Your Source for Latest Celebrity Gossip." Hmm. Gossip doesn't have to be true to be shared. And just because someone gossips about something doesn't mean they're an expert. He's thinking this source is a no-go. But he still wants to finish his questions to make sure.

Nur begins his search. He thought finding a good source for information on Taylor Swift would be easy. He's learning otherwise.

It's important to pay attention to the details when thinking about media. Nur searches for very specific information.

Find out all you can about a source. It may look reliable at first. But don't be afraid to dig deeper.

- **Where did they get their information?**

  Nur again reads the caption under the picture of Taylor Swift. It says, "Swift hints at new album releasing soon." The caption doesn't include "@taylorswift." That's Swift's verified Instagram account. If *Page Eight* isn't including @taylorswift, then maybe Swift doesn't know about the post. There's no source mentioned in the post. The answer to this question has made Nur even more wary of this source.

- **Will this source make money from the content? How does the company or person who made this make their money?**

Nur has seen celebrity magazines at the check-out aisle in the grocery store. He's asked his mom about them. She told him that the magazine companies make more money if they sell more magazines. So they publish anything they can about celebrities, even if it isn't true. It gets people to buy the magazines. He's starting to think this account may be the same. He notices a lot of posts on the page that say, "Click the link in our bio to shop." The pages linked from this profile are full of ads! He knows that companies can make money off ads on their websites. He decides this source is just using Taylor Swift's name to make money. He also thinks that probably means they don't care if the information they post is true.

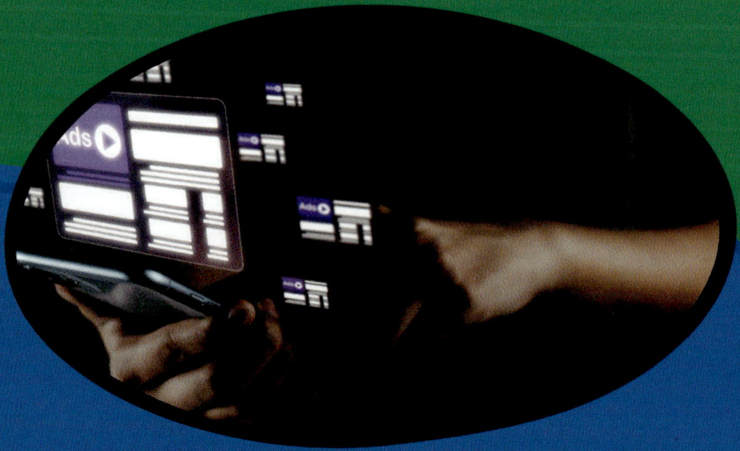

TEEN FACT-CHECKERS TO THE RESCUE!

Interested in identifying sources? Want to **debunk** myths about everything from vaccines to TikTok bans? Teens are doing this in the MediaWise Teen Fact-Checker Network!

MediaWise **correspondents** are middle and high school students who teach others how to spot online fact and fiction. Part of this process includes identifying and learning more about the source. Though it's only *part* of fact-checking, it's an important part!

The correspondents share their findings on YouTube and other social platforms. They use the methods shared in this book to research sources. Beyond that? Fact-checkers also contact any groups or people on which a story focuses. They try to ensure fair and balanced pieces.

Nur's media sleuthing skills led him to a source he trusts.

Nur decides to check out the account @taylorswift. Swifties at his school follow this page. They've told him Taylor Swift posts here. The people who work for her post here. It also has a blue verified checkmark. This source seems much more trustworthy!

After finding a trustworthy source, Nur spends 3 hours reading about Swift's music and current tour. He's glad he didn't just go with the first source he found. He could have embarrassed himself with other Swifties! He'll now have plenty of other Taylor news to talk about.

SHARE & EXPLORE

AI is being used more and more to create images. Work with a friend to try to spot AI-generated photos. See if you can find other images from the same event. Look at the background. Does the location look odd? For images, you can source-trace through reverse searches on Google Lens or TinEye. These steps can keep you and your friend from getting photo-duped.

CHAPTER 3

Show What You Know! Be a Source Sleuth

People share information with you every day. Maybe it's a **viral** photo of a wolf-dog. Or perhaps it's your cousin telling you a Thanksgiving tale about the invention of tofu turkey.

It's important to ask critical questions about *where* information comes from and *how* it changes over time. It's important to recognize that data has an origin story. Try to find its source. Then decide if you trust the source.

Books, newspapers, magazines, and brochures are all media as well. Just because they're not on a screen doesn't mean they're not media!

It's important to think about the motivations behind articles you read in the paper or online.

The process might seem overwhelming. Do you want to research every influencer you follow? Do you want to know the motivations behind every article you read? It's up to you to decide how you approach media. You can use the tools in this book to examine sources. Digging a little deeper and asking the questions from Chapter 2 will help you decide if you can trust a source.

CREATE & CURATE

Do you get most of your information from one place? Broaden your "media diet"! With help from a family member or teacher, search for sources on a topic that represent different points of view. Then compare different sources' coverage of the same topic.

There are many online tools available to help you investigate a source. Other people care about trustworthy sources, too!

If you're still unsure about a source, look at websites like Snopes or PolitiFact. Authors who work for these sites **deconstruct**, or break down, rumors and separate fact from fiction. Maybe the information your source is posting is false. You may not choose to trust them.

Taking these steps helps you be a better media consumer and maker.

BEWARE OF BOTS AND TROLLS

"I saw it on TikTok." "I read it on Facebook." Sometimes adults cite social media as a source. The problem with this? There are lots of bots and trolls on social media.

What does this mean? Bots are AI-programmed social media accounts. Generally, they respond to controversial posts. They're often sponsored by governments. The goal is often to cause political confusion in other countries. Platforms like X—formerly known as Twitter—have a big bot problem. The book *What the Fact?* by Seema Yasmin reports that one in six accounts on the platform are fake.

Trolls are another problem. Trolls are actual people. They are sometimes passionate but misinformed volunteers. They are sometimes hired by people to spread false information. Topics like elections and pandemics are hot topics for trolls. Why? Feelings about these issues are strong. Trolls post content that makes people feel even more passionate about their views and less tolerant of other ideas.

Remind the adults you know to check their information. They can make sure it comes from a reliable source. They can ask the questions posed in this book to evaluate sources. Doing so will help them spot bots and track trolls!

Do More!

Extension Activity

Think about your favorite social media platform. Who or what do you follow most? Is it a funny creator on TikTok? Maybe a makeup influencer. Or a birdwatcher who shares their knowledge of birding. Social media is a part of everyday life.

Go into your social media and look at the last video you shared with a friend. Try out your source-sleuthing on this video. It's good to get in practice! You could choose to use the list of traits Nur used in his Taylor Swift research. You can also start with asking the following questions:

- **Who created the video?**
- **Is "#ad" or "#partnership" anywhere under the video?**
- **Does this creator make money from their videos?**
- **Does this creator have any presence outside of social media?**

Note what you find. Maybe you discovered that the source makes money from video ads. This is good to know! Maybe the source is sharing false information to support their personal goals. You get to decide if you trust the source or not.

Learn More

Book

Yasmin, Seema. *What the Fact? Finding the Truth in All the Noise.* New York City, NY: Simon & Schuster, 2023.

On the Web

Search these online sources with an adult:

- MediaWise—Teen Fact-Checking Network Playlists | YouTube
- PBS Media—Investigate: What IS a reliable source anyway?
- Vassar College—Tips and Tricks for Evaluating Sources
- Wonderopolis.org—How do you know if a source is valid?

Glossary

biases (BIE-uhs-uhz) prejudices in favor of or against a thing, person, or group

correspondents (kor-uh-SPAHN-duhntz) people who contribute news or commentary to a media source

curate (KYUR-ayt) to carefully select

debunk (dee-BUHNK) to expose something as false

deconstruct (dee-kuhn-STRUHKT) to take apart

engineers (en-juh-NEERZ) people who design, build, or maintain machines or structures

media (MEE-dee-uh) means of communicating information to large numbers of people, including television, newspapers, magazines, and radio

source (SORS) a creator or producer of information

stereotypes (STAIR-ee-uh-typz) widely held, oversimplified ideas about a person, group, or thing

viral (VYE-ruhl) information that is quickly spread or shared

Index